T0063025

100 Blessings

BARBARA ANN GAREIS

WestBow
PRESS
A DIVISION OF THOMAS NELSON

Copyright © 2013 Barbara Ann Gareis.

All rights reserved. No part of this book may be used or reproduced by
any means, graphic, electronic, or mechanical, including photocopying,
recording, taping or by any information storage retrieval system
without the written permission of the publisher except in the case
of brief quotations embodied in critical articles and reviews.

Unless otherwise noted, all Scripture quotations are taken from The
Holy Bible, New King James Version. Copyright 1982 by _Thomas Nelson,
Inc._ Used by permission. All rights reserved. Any italics within Bible
quotations have been added by the present author for emphasis.

WestBow Press books may be ordered through booksellers or by contacting:

WestBow Press
A Division of Thomas Nelson
1663 Liberty Drive
Bloomington, IN 47403
www.westbowpress.com
1-(866) 928-1240

Because of the dynamic nature of the Internet, any web addresses or
links contained in this book may have changed since publication and
may no longer be valid. The views expressed in this work are solely those
of the author and do not necessarily reflect the views of the publisher,
and the publisher hereby disclaims any responsibility for them.

Any people depicted in stock imagery provided by Thinkstock are models,
and such images are being used for illustrative purposes only.

Certain stock imagery © Thinkstock.

ISBN: 978-1-4497-9072-1 (sc)
ISBN: 978-1-4497-9073-8 (e)

Library of Congress Control Number: 2013906129

Printed in the United States of America.

WestBow Press rev. date: 4/22/2013

Contents

This book is dedicated to everyone who believed in me, encouraged me, and told me to follow my heart and never give up.

Acknowledgments

The following people are major contributors in helping me launch this book. I am very grateful for their generosity and support:

Charles and Jean Aby

Marylee Beebe

Jen Edwards

Pastor John and Kathleen Goodhart

BillieAnn and Anthony Graiff

Anne LoCastro

Bob and Sandy Nutt

Evelyn and Bernard Nutt

John Lee Roy Parcels Sr.

Jill Lynn Pawlowski

Dale R. Pfost
Vince Vita
David S. Workman
Friends of Shadyrest Bible Church

I want to express my deepest appreciation to my mom, Bernadette Clugsten, for believing in me, for encouraging me, and for setting a wonderful example as a godly woman. Your diligence in daily devotions, church attendance, and praying without ceasing did not go unnoticed.

I also want to thank my husband, George; my daughter, Jessica; and my son, George Jr., for their patience, love, and support throughout this journey.

Thank you to Kickstarter and everyone who supported me through Kickstarter—several of whom I don't know and have never met, but they believed in me and have supported me, and I'm very grateful.

Finally, thank you to my new friends at WestBow Press: Edward Foggs, Barbra Carter, Khristina McKillop, Sam Fitzgerald, and many others who provided feedback, guidance, and assistance to me in preparing this book for publication.

Introduction

I am by no means an expert. I can only share what I know based on experience and what God has laid on my heart to share with you.

I've had many trials in my life, big and small. I've survived illness and injury, bankruptcy and bullying, tragic losses of loved ones, and setbacks that made absolutely no sense to me. My marriage has been a constant challenge, and my career choices have me scratching my head. But through it all, I refuse to give up. I will not quit. I know that I have a purpose here on earth, and I am learning what that is. Some of us know at a very young age that we were born to sing, to practice medicine, to care for children, or to lead a corporation (which can be like caring for children in some cases).

Some of us don't figure out where we belong until we are well into our forties or fifties or even later. I can tell you where you belong. You belong right where you are, at this time and in this place.

I believe there is a season for everything, and there is a reason for everything. Let me say that again. There is a reason for *everything*. That means good, bad, ugly, confusing, difficult, and impossible. We are human. We make mistakes. We make poor choices. We even suffer tragedies that are completely beyond our control. And hopefully we learn something from them.

The Bible even tells us that there is a time for everything. Ecclesiastes 3:1–8 reads:

> To everything there is a season,
> A time for every purpose under heaven:
> A time to be born, and a time to die;
> A time to plant, and a time to pluck what
> is planted;
> A time to kill, and a time to heal;
> A time to break down, and a time to
> build up;
> A time to weep, and a time to laugh;
> A time to mourn, and a time to dance;
> A time to cast away stones, and a time to
> gather stones;

A time to embrace, and a time to refrain
from embracing;
A time to gain, and a time to lose;
A time to keep, and a time to throw
away;
A time to tear, and a time to sew;
A time to keep silence, and a time to
speak;
A time to love, and a time to hate;
A time of war, and a time of peace.

I understand these verses to mean that we will experience all sorts of circumstances in our lifetime. Good things will happen. Bad things will happen. These things will happen at prescribed times—times prescribed by God. We will experience the joys of birth and the sorrows of death. There will be times when doors are closed and others are opened.

We need to be aware of the seasons in our lives and know how best to respond to the circumstances taking place. The only way to do this is to ask God to guide us through these seasons and trust Him in the way that He leads us. We are told that "all things work together for good to those who love God, to those who are the called according to His purpose" (Romans 8:28). What good could possibly come out of thousands of people losing their homes in the fury of a hurricane? Or our teenagers becoming both victims and criminals on our city streets? Or an innocent child killed by a drunk driver? I don't know, and I'm not sure that any of us will ever know the answer to these questions in our lifetime. But we are promised that *all* things work together for good. This may not make sense to us now, but I believe that God uses these events to make us stronger and give us opportunities to prove that we still trust Him.

The devastation after Hurricane Sandy was unbearable. So many families returned home to find a vacant lot. If they were fortunate enough to still have a house, it was ruined by several feet of water, sand, and mold. Many of these homes were demolished or abandoned. Families are now homeless. Life will never be the same for them.

Anyone who has children is all too familiar with the blessing and pain of parenthood twisted together like a vanilla-and-chocolate ice cream cone. One of the greatest joys and challenges in life is becoming a parent. When your baby is placed in your arms and those gentle eyes lock onto your gaze, you're hooked. You suddenly know that without a doubt you would give your life for that child. But raising that child is not easy. For the first few months, you're exhausted. Sometimes you're not sure how this tiny human being can spew milk so far or scream so loudly. During the toddler years, you find yourself covering outlets, locking cabinet doors, and gating off the stairs. I remember when my nephew was happily rolling through the house in his walker and suddenly tumbled end over end down the first flight of steps—only to land upright and still intact. Thank goodness he was okay! I'm not so sure my sister was okay, but fortunately there was no need for a trip to the ER.

Once your child begins school, you pray he or she will be safe and won't be bullied or become lost. When your child becomes a teenager, you have even more to be concerned about—peer pressure, safety on the roads, and nowadays safety in the classroom. Perhaps you have a child with a learning disability, autism, a rare disease, or Down syndrome. If not, you know someone who does. These challenges bring even more confusion, worry, and fear.

God allowed my mom's ten-year-old brother to be hit and killed while riding his bike. He allowed my aunt to die of cancer when she was in her twenties. He took my eighteen-month-old cousin Joey in a house fire and my sixteen-year-old cousin Allen in a car accident. Then He called home my friends Rich and Cindy when they too were in a horrible car accident on their way to Cindy's sister's rehearsal dinner (they were both in the wedding party, the wedding that was taking place the following day). He also took my dad at the young age of forty-five after a months-long battle with cancer. It's very difficult to emotionally and philosophically maneuver through these painful events.

Yes, God allowed these things to happen. More important, God also understands our pain. After all, He watched His own Son take His last breath as He hung on a cross, nails piercing His hands and feet, a crown of thorns around His head. He was surrounded by people who spat at Him and cursed His name. He did this for us, and for that, we are to praise Him and trust Him to see us through trying times.

Even the little things in life can be trying, especially when they start accumulating. The house always needs work. There's never enough money in the bank account to pay all the bills. The kids are sick. The job you once loved has become stressful, no longer enjoyable. The car is in the shop every other week. The dog peed on the rug. The coffeepot won't work (yes, for me that is a tragedy). The list goes on. Before you know it, the bumps in the road feel like mountains. But the Bible says in Philippians 4:11, "Not that I speak in regard to need, for I have learned in whatever state I am, to be content." What? I'm supposed to be content when my life feels like it's falling apart? Yes. Yes, I am. An elderly poet in Psalm 71:6, 8 says, "My praise shall be continually of You" and "Let my mouth be filled with Your praise and with Your glory all the day." Regardless of what this man was going through, He continued to praise God. He trusted Him.

In the movie *Facing the Giants*, a high school football team has not won a game in six consecutive seasons. The team's coach is sure things can't get any worse, but he's wrong. With every area of his life falling apart, Coach Grant Taylor turns to God in desperation. He believes that through trust in God, anything is possible. He and his team make a promise that no matter what happens, they will glorify God. Their newfound faith proves that "with God all things are possible" (see Mark 10:27).

We also aren't supposed to wait for God to do something good before we praise Him. We are to praise Him in all circumstances and then let Him show us His goodness, which He weaves throughout all of life's prickly vines. I understand this isn't easy, but it is commanded of us and it is necessary for survival in this world we live in.

Trials, Tragedies, and Tears

Early in my marriage, when my husband and I had a disagreement, he would say, "Remember, it takes a little rain to make love grow." He was right. We cannot grow a garden full of beautiful lilies, roses, and tulips without dirt, rain, and fertilizer. We cannot get an education without attending classes, studying hard, and completing our assignments. And we cannot build a beautiful house without bricks, wood, nails, and sweat. The same goes for life in general. We cannot become loving, caring, faithful people without enduring the trials that naturally come our way throughout our time here on earth.

Romans 8:28 says, "We know that all things work together for good to those who love God, to those who are the called according to His purpose." The Bible says that *all* things work together for good. *All* means "all." It means health and illness, birth and death, wealth and poverty. How can so many bad things in the world work together for *good*? Only God knows that answer. But I believe it to be true, and I believe we will see this proof either here on earth at a later time or when we all get to heaven.

Sometimes I try to figure out what good things have come out of the difficulties in my past. For instance, my dad died when he was only forty-five years old, and I've wondered (naturally) what good could possibly come from this. I could be wrong, but I like to think that the shock of my sister's pregnancy at sixteen years old worked for good in that my dad was able to experience the joy of a grandchild for a short time before his death.

Also, getting married at the age of twenty is not something I recommend. I am still married to the same man, but our marriage has not been easy (and I know that most marriages do take a lot of work). At twenty years old, you really have not begun to figure out who you are or what life is all about yet. The good that came from this is not only my husband and our two wonderful children, whom I love more than anything in the world, but the fact that my dad was able to walk me down the aisle on my wedding day, and I was able to enjoy that cherished father–daughter dance at our reception.

Maybe some good that came from his death is that we are a small step closer to finding the cure for cancer. When chemotherapy was no longer working for him, he agreed to try an experimental cancer drug. I remember him saying, "If it will help cancer research so that there will someday be a cure and children will no longer have to suffer with cancer like I am, then I want to do it." The experimental drug did not help him, but perhaps it helped researchers to understand what they needed to do next to continue searching for the cure.

I also like to think that because I experienced the loss of a parent at such a young age, I might be able to comfort someone else in a similar situation because I understand what that person is going through. It doesn't make the pain of missing my dad go away, but I know that I'm able to be there for others during their time of grieving too, and that knowledge is a comfort.

Another personal trial that I recall is when I was taken to the hospital and admitted for a week because of a severe allergic reaction to a vaccine. I had developed a fever, chills, a rash, and dizziness, and eventually I passed out. After I regained consciousness, my husband took me to the doctor. My blood sugar was extremely high, and I was still very weak and dizzy, so my doctor had an ambulance take me to the hospital. After some blood work and other tests, they decided I needed to stay.

Anyone who knows me knows I am not one to sit still, and here I was in a hospital bed attached to a heart monitor and an IV, with a snarl of wires connected to me. I was forced to do nothing. I was frustrated. Looking back, I think perhaps this was God's way of making me sit still, get the rest that I desperately needed, and reflect on His plan for me and my future. I would not have done it on my own. I needed Him to force me to be still.

I was also blessed to have the nicest doctors and nurses on staff and an even nicer roommate. My roommate was much older; in fact, she was twice my age. And she was scared. There were moments when I reassured her she would be okay, and there were other moments when she reassured me. We talked quite a bit about our families and life in general. She met my friends and family who came to visit, and I met hers. There's a reason we were in that room together, even if it was simply to reassure one another. I think of her from time to time and wonder what became of her. And I thank God for putting her in my life even if for only a week.

I have many stories like this, as I'm sure you do too. Even Dave Ramsey would probably agree that all things work together for good. At twenty-six years old, he was already a millionaire but accumulated so much debt that he lost everything. Perhaps the good that came out of this was that he learned (the hard way) the importance of managing money properly, and now he is able to help others do the same through his *Total Money Makeover* and *Financial Peace* programs.

I like to think of this scenario as paying it forward. If each and every one of us could learn one thing from a difficult situation and then help someone else get through that same situation, we would all be paying it forward and making the world a better place. Remember, there is a reason for everything. How can you positively impact someone's life with what *you've* experienced?

Another profound verse is Hebrews 13:5, which reads, "Let your conduct be without covetousness; be content with such things as you have. For He Himself has said, 'I will never leave you nor forsake you.'" There are two parts to this verse. First, we are told to be content with what we have. This is not easy. I know. I have struggled with this many times myself. It is extremely difficult to be content when we try so hard to do what's right and when we work so hard to make ends meet, and it still feels as though our world is caving in around us. How is a cancer patient supposed to be content in her situation? How is a homeless man supposed to be content living on a cold sidewalk? But contentment does not always have to do with our surroundings, our physical well-being, or our means of shelter (or lack thereof). Contentment comes from the heart. We must be content with who we are, what we believe, and how we live.

The second part of this verse is what we must remind ourselves of every single day. He will never leave us or forsake us. There might be times when it feels like God has left us. I have cried out on more than one occasion, "God, where are you? Why aren't you here? You said you would never leave me, so why do I feel so alone?" Trust me. He is with us, and He hears us—always. He answers every single prayer. Sometimes the answers aren't what we expect, but He knows what's best for us, and we need to trust Him with what He gives us (or doesn't give us). Our own friends and family will disappoint us. They will reject us, abandon us, and hurt us. But God is one Friend who will never reject us, abandon us, or hurt us. Although we cannot see Him in the physical sense, or even hear him audibly, He is always with us, and we should take comfort in knowing that.

Perhaps you feel you have every right to grumble and complain about your circumstances. That's okay. Find a quiet place where you can be alone. Cry. Complain. Throw something. Even yell at God. It's okay. Then after a few minutes, or a few months, be still and pray. Pray that God will show you how to handle what you're going through. Pray that you will learn something from this experience so that you can help others. Thank Him for being with you through this difficulty you are experiencing—because He is. Then listen, and follow your heart.

We all need God in our lives, and we all need one another in some way. You've heard the phrase, "Man cannot live on bread alone." It's true. We need God, and we need one another. We need to feel loved, encouraged, and supported. We need to know that others have walked in our shoes. We need to pick ourselves up (with God's help, of course), brush ourselves off, and look for ways to share peace, love, and kindness in this ever-challenging and confusing world.

I don't have all the answers, and I never will. I can't justify the Columbine High School massacre, or the Virginia Tech murders, or the death of twenty children and six adults at the hands of one deranged man in a Connecticut elementary school. There are monsters in this world, and the only sense of understanding I have for this most recent tragic event can also be found in the Bible. There are four parts to what I've recently learned about this tragedy as well as other tragedies that sadly take place daily all around the world.

Part 1: How God Feels about Children

Matthew 18:1–5 reads,

> At that time the disciples came to Jesus, saying, "Who then is greatest in the kingdom of heaven?"
>
> Then Jesus called a little child to Him, set him in the midst of them, and said, "Assuredly, I say to you, unless you are converted and become as little children, you will by no means enter the kingdom of heaven. Therefore whoever humbles himself as this little child is the greatest in the kingdom of heaven. Whoever receives one little child like this in My name receives Me."

It is evident that God loves our children and has prepared a special place for them in heaven. When I was a little girl, I had a Bible with a picture on the cover of Jesus surrounded by children. He had children in His lap and sitting at His feet. His eyes were gentle, and He was focused on them with complete adoration. I used to stare at this picture and run my fingers over the leather cover, imagining what it must be like to be in the presence of the Lord as a young child.

He certainly cares for the little ones, as mentioned in several places throughout the Bible. Proverbs 22:6 gives instructions on how to raise up our children. Psalm 127:3 speaks of children being a heritage from the Lord. Children are a gift, a blessing, from God. Psalm 128 is a story of "building" sons and daughters. We as parents (grandparents, aunts, uncles, or caregivers) are to instill faith in our children at a very young age. We are to pray for them and teach them God's Word, thus laying a foundation for their future. They are the most valuable blessing we could ever hope for.

John 1:12 speaks of His believers being His children. It reads, "As many as received Him, to them He gave the right to become children of God, to those who believe in His name." We know how much we love our children, so imagine how much God loves us and our children. I have a great peace in knowing that the little ones in my family—Russy (age two years), Joey (eighteen months), and Danny (one day)—are in heaven today.

Part 2: God's Warning

Matthew 18:6 reads, "Whoever causes one of these little ones who believe in Me to sin, it would be better for him if a millstone were hung around his neck, and he were drowned in the depth of the sea." A millstone is a large round stone used for grinding grain. Imagine how heavy a millstone must be. God warns that those who devalue the little children deserve to have this heavy stone attached to them and be thrown into the sea for certain drowning. This is punishment that God Himself says is appropriate for those who harm our children—it is, in fact, lighter than the punishment that awaits them spiritually.

The next verse continues, "Woe to the world because of offenses! For offenses must come, but woe to that man by whom the offense comes!" First, He says that offenses will come (not *might* but *must*). He doesn't promise us a life of roses. He warns us that attacks against us are certain. It does not matter who we are or what we do. He tells us these attacks must come. They must come because man has been given free will to choose how he behaves. Some will choose evil. "Woe to the world" likely means that we all influence each other, whether in a good way or bad way. Those who are evil will (unfortunately) influence others to also do evil.

Second, it again seems clear to me that God will severely punish anyone who offends our children. Jesus goes on to say that our offenses begin in the heart, and we are to cut out of our lives anything that causes us or others to commit the offenses He warns us about. Those who do commit these offenses will have to answer to God one day. He is our ultimate judge, and we will either be rewarded or punished for our actions here on earth.

So why do these tragedies even take place? Why would someone want to hurt our children? That brings me to the next part.

Part 3: We Have No Fear of God

Romans 3:18 reads, "There is no fear of God before their eyes." In this verse, *fear* does not mean being afraid or scared, although it could, as I'll mention later. It primarily means reverent respect. Fearing God in this sense is the foundation for wisdom. We cannot even begin to be obedient to God if we don't first have wisdom.

Fearing God also goes hand in hand with loving Him. This necessary foundation is mentioned throughout the Old Testament. For example, Deuteronomy 10:12 reads, "And now, Israel, what does the Lord your God require of you, but to fear the Lord your God, to walk in all His ways and to love Him, to serve the Lord your God with all your heart and with all your soul …"

The other definition of fearing God is similar to being afraid in that we gain an understanding of how much God hates sin, and this prevents us from doing wrong, much the way we expect our children to have a fear of discipline that prevents them from doing wrong. They don't want to disappoint us, and we should not want to disappoint the One who has created us and loves us.

So fear in the biblical sense means submissive reverence, and to refuse this act is to do things our own way. Those who fear God are blessed with goodness, riches, honor, satisfaction, good relationships with others, a long life, mercy, strong confidence, and God's constant attention. Those who do not fear God are lost and will continue to do things their way by harming others through disrespect, disobedience, injury, and murder.

In the New Testament there is great emphasis on having a gentle and quiet spirit, which is tightly linked to fearing God. First Peter 3:4 tells us, "rather let it [your adornment] be the hidden person of the heart, with the incorruptible beauty of a gentle and quiet spirit, which is very precious in the sight of God." Fearing God will manifest a gentle and quiet spirit within us.

Loving God produces love within us. We cannot begin to love one another without first building a foundation based on the truths and love of God. We start with fearing Him, and the rest falls into place. This progression leads us to part 4.

Part 4: What Happens When We Praise Him

Psalm 111:10 promises, "The fear of the Lord is the beginning of wisdom; a good understanding have all those who do His commandments. His praise endures forever." Praise is simply adoration from the heart. It's not something that comes naturally. It takes practice and trust. The more you praise Him, the more natural it will feel. I wasn't even sure how to praise God when I first became a believer except to thank Him for all that I had each time I prayed. Over time I learned that music is another great way to praise Him, whether we are singing the hymns in church or listening to music that glorifies Him. I am grateful for a wide variety of uplifting music. When I was very young, the only Christian music I was aware of was the hymns we sang in church. Now we have many styles of music to choose from, such as the traditional hymns, praise and worship songs, contemporary music like that of Barlow Girl, MercyMe, Kutless, and Skillet (among many, many other wonderful groups), and even the more energetic music of groups like Flyleaf. If you are interested in learning about this wide variety of styles in Christian music, I recommend you visit www.todayschristianmusic.com.

Praise also keeps Satan from destroying you. Every time you praise God, you beat Satan, and every time you beat Satan, you have more reason to praise God. Praise must be genuine, though, and in time it will be. You will eventually be able to praise Him from your heart even during the most difficult circumstances.

Robbie Parker spoke on national television about the loss of his daughter Emily during the shooting at Sandy Hook Elementary School. He demonstrated his praise of God when he declared forgiveness for what happened. My aunt Sandy and uncle Bob are another example of God-fearing people. They experienced indescribable pain as they mourned the loss of their sixteen-year-old son (my cousin), Allen, when he was killed in a car accident. Yet they forgave the driver, who happened to be Allen's girlfriend, and wrapped their loving arms around her the way our heavenly Father wraps His arms around us. They never wavered in their faith. They use this tragedy for good by ministering to others who are grieving and lost.

We know there will continue to be trials, tragedies, and tears during our lives here on earth, but it is much easier to navigate through these difficulties when we know God is on our side. We just have to trust in Him and stay close to Him. We may at times drift away from Him, but He never moves away from us—ever. And He welcomes us back time and time again with open arms.

Feeling Discouraged

Some days we face major discouragement. Perhaps you've received unfortunate news from a doctor, you were laid off from your job, or you just received a foreclosure notice in the mail. Other days it's the little things that get us down: you spill coffee down the front of your shirt or the babysitter is late or the car won't start.

One particular chilly, dreary day I sat in my parked car during my lunch break eating a ham and cheese sandwich. I was thinking about my boring job, my unfinished education, and my depressing financial situation. I hadn't been sleeping well, I was working too much but barely making ends meet, and I was missing my family. A single teardrop splattered on the wrapper in my lap. Just beyond the wrapper, the gas gauge caught my attention. The needle was on empty, and I was nowhere near a gas station.

It was at this moment that I put my hands up, looked at the gray sky, and said, "God, I cannot do this anymore. I'm giving it all to you. I'm broken. I'm tired. I'm done." More tears began to fall as I pleaded for guidance. Then I heard that little voice in my head: "My child, I am with you. I will never leave you. I have bigger plans for you, and I need you to trust me. Don't waste another minute worrying. Have I not provided for you in the past? During challenges in the workplace? During illnesses? And what about all the loved ones you've lost? Have I not given you the strength and the hope you needed to get through those difficult times? I will carry you through this trial as well."

Just then Carrie Underwood's song "Jesus, Take the Wheel" began playing on the radio. If that's not God's way of showing me He is really with me, I don't know what is. I finally decided I was not going to take control anymore. I was willing to let go.

I thought back to another time when I felt discouraged. Our daughter was three, and we were expecting our second child. Our daughter had been premature, so my second pregnancy was automatically considered high-risk since the chances of another premature delivery were quite high. At twenty weeks' gestation, I was taken out of work and put on bed rest. We could not afford to keep our daughter in day care since I was collecting disability, which was only a fraction of my typical income, and like most people, we were living paycheck to paycheck. So I kept her home with me. If you know any three-year-olds, you know that they do not sit still for very long. There I was on bed rest with an energetic little girl who wanted to jump rope, play on the swings, and run. On top of that, it was spring, so most days the weather was warm, about seventy degrees, and the sun was shining. I had to come up with other ideas for keeping her occupied. We colored pictures in her Bambi coloring book, and we watched *Dumbo* probably three times every day for weeks.

I was uncomfortable, bored, frustrated, and feeling guilty, but with God's help, we persevered. On June 26, 1996, I once again gave birth to another premature baby. Our son was not as tiny as our daughter (she was only 4 pounds 13 ounces, and he was 5 pounds 4 ounces), but he had more obstacles to overcome than she did. He did not have a sucking reflex yet, so he was fed through a tube in his nose. He also developed sleep apnea and had to be on a monitor constantly so that when he stopped breathing, an alarm would sound, and the nurses could attend to him and get him breathing again.

I vividly remember sitting in a rocking chair in the NICU, holding him, and thinking, *He's two weeks old already, and we're still here. It feels like he's been here forever.* I missed my daughter. It was a challenge trying to divide my time between our three-year-old little girl and our newborn preemie in the hospital.

I heard that same voice in my head on that day too. He said, "You have so little faith. Did I not strengthen your little girl and allow you to take her home? I will do the same with your little boy too. Be patient, and trust Me."

I became lost in our son's big blue eyes and prayed, "I trust You."

The following day, the head nurse announced that our baby boy was being discharged and we could finally take him home. I thanked God with all my heart and prayed for the other babies in the NICU and their mommies and daddies, that they could all be together soon too.

Although I was thrilled at having another child, it was a trying time in my life, and I felt discouraged on many days. With the support of my family and friends and my church, I learned to trust God again. He was there with me every step of the way, and together we got through it. My kids have grown to be healthy, happy, thriving individuals.

Other instances began flooding my mind as I was sitting there in the car, like when our son was two years old and had outgrown his clothes. We could barely afford to put food on the table, let alone buy new clothes every time he had another growth spurt. He was wearing a 2T at the time, and I didn't know anyone else who had children his size, so hand-me-downs weren't even an option.

Then one day a friend of my husband's unexpectedly stopped by with his wife. They "just happened to be in the area" and wanted to say hello. As we were talking, his wife asked, "You have a little boy now too, right?" When I replied that we did (he was napping), her eyes lit up, and she led me to the trunk of their car. "Would you be interested in some little boys' underwear? My husband did some shopping last week while I was sick, and he bought the wrong size for our son. They are a 2T." She didn't want me to pay her for them and wasn't planning to return anything to the store. She simply handed me the bags and said she was glad we could use them. If God can answer prayers through little boys' underwear, He can do much more!

Several years later, when my husband was out of work, all we could afford to eat was pancakes for dinner (it seems we were always struggling financially). Our furnace wasn't working properly and needed to be repaired because it was the middle of winter. I made a very difficult decision to cash in some gold. I didn't have much. In fact, all I had was a gold anklet made up of little gold hearts. I treasured this anklet, but I knew it was real gold, and I knew gold was worth something. I had heard an ad on the radio for a guy who paid cash for gold. I looked up the information on the radio station's website and wrote a letter explaining our predicament. I wasn't sure how much the anklet was worth but knew that any little bit would help with the cost of the repair we needed to make. I sealed the envelope that contained my letter and my gold anklet and placed it in the mailbox.

About a week later, I received an envelope in the mail. I ripped it open. The enclosed note read, "Dear Barbara, my wife and I decided to bless you as God has blessed us. We want you to keep your anklet as a reminder of God's love for you. Please accept this gift. We pray that you will be at peace during this difficult time." I tipped the envelope to one side, and out slid my gold anklet and three hundred dollars in cash. Now each time I open my Bible and see that handwritten note tucked inside the back cover, I am reminded of God's provision, and each time I wear the gold anklet with the little hearts, I am reminded of God's love.

The sun over the parking lot had shifted just enough that the glare off the window snapped me back to the present day. There were so many times over the years when I felt discouraged, depressed, and done. And each time, the Lord proved that He was real. How could I not trust Him yet again?

So I challenged myself to think of ten things in my life that I am thankful for. I turned off my cell phone to avoid any distractions, took pen and paper, and jotted down a few of the blessings in my life. After several minutes, I had written down about fifteen little things I was thankful for. I checked the time and realized my lunch hour was up, so I set my notebook aside and returned to the office. But I was not finished with this challenge. Later that afternoon, I remembered something else I was thankful for, so I made a quick note of it. When my workday ended, I made a quick stop at a gas station that fortunately wasn't as far away as I thought, and I continued driving home. Along the way, I thought of a few more blessings in my life. When I arrived home, I took out my notebook and added those items to my list as well.

This little endeavor was beginning to cheer me up. I then decided to challenge myself to list a hundred blessings in my life. I continued to add to my list, and in less than twenty-four hours, I had exceeded my goal. To this day, I am still adding blessings to the list.

I share this story with you because we have all been there. We get discouraged. We face trials and tribulations, sometimes for weeks or even months at a time. I encourage you to list one hundred blessings of your own. I'm sharing my own list with you to give you ideas. You might have many of the same blessings, and some might cause you to think of other blessings in your life that aren't in my list. Some of my blessings may seem odd, but each and every one has special meaning to me, and I think you'll find the same as you begin to make your list too.

This little activity does not mean the difficulties you are facing will magically disappear, but I promise it will put a smile on your face and give you some sense of peace, hope, and happiness. Keep it, add to it, and read it over and over again as a reminder that He will never leave you or forsake you.

Barbara Gareis's 100 Blessings

1. The sweet smell of fresh-cut grass on a warm spring day
2. Warm and gooey fresh-baked cookies just out of the oven
3. A baby's smile
4. The first flowers of spring
5. A quiet snowfall
6. A cat's purr
7. A puppy's breath
8. Advances in technology
9. The ability to walk, talk, see, hear, smell, touch, and love
10. Freedom
11. A warm blanket

12. A crackling fire
13. Well-written books
14. My Bible
15. Best friends
16. Choices
17. Opportunities
18. A child's first haircut
19. An education
20. Love letters
21. Graduation
22. A variety of music
23. The nativity scene
24. Simplicity
25. Doctors and medicine
26. Watermelon
27. Majestic mountains
28. Sparkling lakes
29. A beautiful sunrise
30. A beautiful sunset
31. Birds chirping on a spring morning
32. The changing color of leaves in the fall
33. Board games
34. A good movie
35. Laughter
36. Planes, trains, and automobiles
37. Horse-drawn carriage rides

38. Class reunions
39. Communion
40. Soft grass under my bare feet
41. The aroma of hot asphalt
42. A cool swimming pool on a hot day
43. A pond full of colorful fish
44. Lazy days
45. Rainy days
46. Napping in a hammock under a shady tree
47. Positive self-talk
48. A sincere compliment, both given and received
49. Entrepreneurship
50. A child's innocence
51. Lip balm
52. Tears of joy
53. Catching all green lights
54. Catching fireflies on a warm summer night
55. Butterflies
56. White clouds against a blue sky
57. Hopscotch
58. Cookie dough
59. The smile on my face as I'm writing this list
60. Soap and warm water
61. A bubble bath
62. Discovering a hidden talent
63. Jigsaw puzzles

64. The hatching of a baby chick
65. Words of encouragement
66. The fragrance of a summer rain
67. Inspiring stories
68. Sun-brewed iced tea
69. Hugs from an old friend
70. A good listener
71. A plush bathrobe
72. Our servicemen and -women
73. Caregivers
74. Charity
75. Soup kitchens
76. Sandpipers
77. Efforts to find a cure for cancer
78. A stranger's smile
79. Childbirth
80. Rainbows
81. Museums
82. Freshly sharpened pencils
83. Back-to-school days
84. Sweatpants and sneakers
85. S'mores
86. A rustic campsite
87. Sailboats
88. The face of a koala bear
89. Classic Christmas shows

90. Times Square

91. Hand sanitizer

92. A toddler's first steps

93. The elderly

94. Firefighters and police officers

95. Volunteers

96. Calculators

97. The sound of crashing waves

98. Pink sand

99. Seashells

100. A hayride and pumpkin picking

I hope this list will put a smile on your face as it did mine. In the appendix you will find space to list your own blessings. I know you will be able to think of lots of blessings in your life as well.

Don't give up. Don't quit. Give yourself a break, and remind yourself every day of all the things you have to be thankful for.

The Greatest Blessing

There is one more blessing I did not include in my list. That is because it is far more important than any other blessing and deserves a special place, not a number. This blessing is forgiveness.

None of us is perfect. We are human. We are born with sin. We make mistakes. We break promises. We hurt others' feelings. We say things we don't mean. We hold grudges. We become resentful and bitter. We lie, cheat, and steal. We commit adultery and murder. We allow anger to eat away at us like rust eats away metal. This is not how God wants us to live, yet He forgives us. And we are to forgive one another. He sent His Son, Jesus, to die on the cross to forgive us of our sins so that we can have eternal life. God's forgiveness is complete.

If God can forgive us, how can we not forgive each other or even ourselves? In fact, forgiveness here on earth is a prerequisite for receiving God's forgiveness. And God doesn't expect us to forgive a person once. We are to forgive him or her as many times as needed.

Peter approached Jesus and asked in Matthew 18:21, "Lord, how often shall my brother sin against me, and I forgive him? Up to seven times?"

Jesus' reply (verse 22) was, "I do not say to you, up to seven times, but up to seventy times seven." In other words, as many times as you have been wronged, that's how many times you are to forgive. *Every* time.

Ephesians 4:32 is a well-known verse and reminds us to "be kind to one another, tenderhearted, forgiving one another, even as God in Christ forgave you." And Colossians 3:12–13 tells us, "Therefore, as the elect of God, holy and beloved, put on tender mercies, kindness, humility, meekness, longsuffering; bearing with one another, and forgiving one another, if anyone has a complaint against another; even as Christ forgave you, so you also must do."

Forgiveness is not an option. It is a requirement. It is also an act of obedience. If you wait until you feel like forgiving, it will never happen. You need to forgive regardless of how you feel. If you are willing to forgive, God will give you the right words to say, and He will equip you to follow through. Forgiveness does not mean that you accept or excuse the wrong that was done, but it does bring freedom, God's blessings, and goodness.

Hope, Strength, and Comfort

My Bible has a sidebar on each page with notes that expound upon many of the verses. The title in my Bible for Romans 5:1–5 is "Faith Triumphs in Trouble." The sidebar note reads, "The believer receives a new relationship with God, a new perspective on difficulty, and a new assurance of security."

The first four verses read, "Therefore, having been justified by faith, we have peace with God through our Lord Jesus Christ, through whom also we have access by faith into this grace in which we stand, and rejoice in hope of the glory of God. And not only that, but we also glory in tribulations, knowing that tribulation produces perseverance; and perseverance, character; and character, hope." Verse 5 continues, "Now *hope* does not disappoint, because the love of God has been poured out in our hearts by the Holy Spirit who was given to us."

I believe there are benefits to be gained when we respond properly to suffering. Pressures produce perseverance. When we think of rain and mud, we tend to feel gloomy. But think about the beauty of a garden, as I mentioned earlier. The colorful flowers surrounded by all the greenery would not be possible without plenty of dirt and rain. The same is true in our lives. Tribulations are necessary for our growth. As the verse above stated, tribulation produces perseverance, which produces character, which produces hope.

And what exactly is hope? *Webster's* defines it as a desire with expectation of fulfillment. How exciting is it that we can desire a future that God promises, and we can expect it to be fulfilled because He tells us it will be?

When I was a little girl, I listened intently as my Sunday school teacher told me the story of Jesus—how He was born of the Virgin Mary and later died on the cross to wash away our sins because He loves us that much. She explained that, if we accept Him into our hearts, we will go to heaven when we die. She shared the story of hope. I clung to it, and she prayed with me so that I could know without a doubt that one day I would go to heaven. I've hung on to this hope all my life, and despite the thorns that scratch me as I walk along the path of life, I still persevere. I press forward because I have the hope that has been promised to me. It's promised to you too if you accept it.

Psalm 27:1 reads, "The Lord is my light and my salvation; whom shall I fear? The Lord is the *strength* of my life; of whom shall I be afraid?" The presence of God in our lives gives us inner resources to overcome fear in difficult situations.

Psalm 46:1 reads, "God is our refuge and *strength*, a very present help in trouble." The psalmist who wrote this was believed to have been in the midst of troublesome times, yet he was confident in his faith and made this known. Another verse regarding strength is Isaiah 40:31: "Those who wait on the Lord shall renew their *strength*; they shall mount up with wings like eagles, they shall run and not be weary, they shall walk and not faint." Read this verse again, and this time, substitute the word *wings* with *faith*. "But those who wait on the Lord shall renew their *strength*; they shall mount up with faith like eagles, they shall run and not be weary, they shall walk and not faint." Did you know that storms allow eagles to fly higher? Imagine the faith of an eagle as it soars above the storms in our skies. If only we had that same measure of faith during the storms we face in our lifetime.

When we are overburdened, we get tired and weak. We feel like we can't go on. Most of us have heard the poem "Footprints in the Sand." It goes like this:

> One night a man had a dream. He dreamed he was walking along the beach with the Lord.
> Across the sky flashed scenes from his life.
> For each scene he noticed two sets of footprints in the sand: one belonging to him, and the other to the Lord.
> When the last scene of his life flashed before him, he looked back at the footprints in the sand.
> He noticed that many times along the path of his life there was only one set of footprints.
> He also noticed that it happened at the very lowest and saddest times in his life.
> This really bothered him and he questioned the Lord about it:

"Lord, you said that once I decided to
follow you, you'd walk with me all the
way.
But I have noticed that during the most
troublesome times in my life, there is
only one set of footprints.
I don't understand why when I needed
you most you would leave me."
The Lord replied:
"My son, my precious child,
I love you and I would never leave you.
During your times of trial and suffering,
when you see only one set of footprints,
it was then that I carried you."

The most popular Sunday school song I know is
about the strength of Jesus. I must have sung it a hundred
times when I was little. The song starts out, "Jesus loves
me! This I know, for the Bible tells me so. Little ones to
Him belong; they are weak, but He is strong." When we
are weak, he is strong. He will carry us.

One of the best-known passages in the Bible, Psalm 23,
speaks of comfort. Verse 4 reads, "Yea, though I walk
through the valley of the shadow of death, I will fear no
evil; for You are with me, Your rod and Your staff, they

comfort me." This verse promises that God will protect us and comfort us when we walk through the valleys (the low times in our lives, the difficulties). Isaiah 51:12 starts off with "I, even I, am He who *comforts* you." This is God promising His people that He would comfort them, and He still does this today.

Finally, in order for us as believers to grow in our faith, we must comfort one another by showing love and encouragement, as commanded in 1 Thessalonians 5:11: "*Comfort* each other and edify one another, just as you also are doing."

When my dad was battling cancer, my family was comforted by people who prayed for us, visited us, made us meals, ran errands for us, hugged us, and simply sat with us in silence. For weeks and even months after he lost his fight, we continued to be comforted by phone calls, cards, hymns, and the mere presence of friends and family—and of course the comfort we have in our faith in God.

We are going to go through difficult circumstances. We will get sick. We will lose loved ones. We will face conflict. There are so many situations that we and those we are closest to are facing that I cannot even begin to list them all here on these pages. But no matter how bad things get, do not give up. Do not quit. We have a wonderful, loving God who wants us to go to Him when we need help. He will carry us through every situation we are facing now and will face in the future. He loves us more than we could possibly love another human being. This is something we cannot even comprehend. Just give it all to Him, and let Him lead the way.

Suffering and Blessing of Job

Before I share the story of Job, I need to tell you how I learned about the story of Job. It was October 2008.

I had always had a small mole near my left knee, and I had noticed it was getting gradually larger, but it still was no bigger than a pencil eraser. I also noticed the shape was no longer round. It was becoming asymmetrical. Still I didn't think much of it until my husband walked into the room and asked what was on my leg. I was sitting on the bed in a pair of shorts and a T-shirt with a book propped up on my pillow. The fact that he noticed something different enough to point it out from across the room prompted me to call the dermatologist the next day and make an appointment.

The dermatologist agreed it didn't look normal, so she took a scraping and sent it to the lab to be biopsied. While waiting about a week for the results, I of course tried to diagnose myself by searching every site on the Internet about skin cancer. I looked at hundreds of images trying to find a picture that matched the mole my doctor had removed. I read all about actinic keratosis, basal cell carcinoma, dysplastic nevi, squamous cell carcinoma, and the worst—malignant melanoma. I was sure I didn't have the worst kind, although the images looked quite similar.

Before I continue, though, I must tell you my complexion is very fair, and as a teenager I purposely baked myself under the sun. The highest protection available back then was SPF 8, but even that I felt was too much. I wanted a tan. Isn't that what makes us beautiful? I knew that with my fair complexion I would burn, but eventually my red skin would become tan, and the pain would be worth it. My friends and I would slather on the baby oil and fry ourselves for hours, like rotisserie chickens that were basted and turned regularly in order to perfect their crispy brown skin.

There were days when I could not even get out of bed the next morning; when I tried to stand up, the slightest pressure of putting weight on my sunburned legs would cause excruciating pain, like being stabbed with thousands of knives all at once. I remember missing school because of my sunburn and even crawling across the hall from my bedroom to the bathroom because I couldn't walk. Whatever skin didn't blister eventually tanned in about a week or two. Now, twenty years later, I was reading about how it can take up to twenty years for cancer to develop if you did not protect your skin from the harmful rays.

As I waited for the news, my heart skipped a beat each time the phone rang. Finally my doctor called my cell phone while I was at work. When she asked, "Do you have a few minutes to talk?" I knew it wasn't good news. I think I only heard every other word but caught the important ones like "cancer … caught early … schedule surgery … melanoma." Wait. Melanoma? Did she just say "melanoma"?

I hung up the phone and sat down in an empty conference room all alone. Fear washed over me, the way a tsunami strikes without warning. I knew the spot on my leg was small, but I had read and heard of people who died from melanoma. I began to cry and didn't know what to do first. Tell my boss? Call my husband? Take a walk? I said a prayer. Then I called my husband and my mom. I finished out the workday barely able to concentrate on whatever I was doing.

Outpatient surgery was scheduled to remove the area that was biopsied. I was told they would cut a small area out of my thigh and suture it. They would do another biopsy to be sure they had removed all the cancerous cells. After a couple of weeks they would remove the sutures, and I would need to have a body scan every few months. My doctor also stressed the importance of using the highest SPF available from now on and staying out of the sun as much as possible.

A few days after the surgery, I went to my son's football game. While other moms basked in the sun along the sidelines, I sat in the bleachers wearing a long-sleeved shirt and held an umbrella over my head to shield myself from the rays of cancer. A few days before I was to have the sutures removed, my dermatologist called me again. She explained that they would not be removing the sutures. The biopsy showed they did not get all the cancerous cells, and they would need to remove a larger area. In other words, they would be cutting out the area that was sutured and then some.

I wanted to scream. *Why? When will this be over? How many more times will they need to cut me? What if they don't get it all this time? Will I need chemo? Am I going to die?* I knew melanoma was deadly, and that wave of fear washed over me again.

I prayed again. This time out of nowhere the word *Job* popped into my mind. I had heard Bible stories of Job in church before but had never actually read the book myself. That afternoon I opened my Bible to the book of Job and began to read.

Job lived a prosperous life and was a righteous man who loved the Lord. He was blameless and honest. He feared God and did all he could to avoid evil people and things. He and his wife had seven sons and three daughters. Job's possessions included thousands of animals, a large household, and many servants. They had plenty of food and feasted regularly. He was an early riser and offered burnt offerings to the Lord regularly. One day when his sons and daughters were enjoying a meal together, a messenger approached Job and announced that they had been raided. The oxen and donkeys were taken, and the servants were killed. During this announcement, another messenger came and said that fire fell from the sky and burned up the sheep and the servants with them. A third messenger came to announce that the camels were also taken, and more servants were killed. Then a fourth messenger came to exclaim that a great wind from the wilderness had destroyed the house where his sons and daughters were eating and drinking. They were killed when the house fell upon them.

Job tore off his robe, shaved his head, fell to his knees, and worshipped God, saying in Job 1:21, "Naked I came from my mother's womb, and naked shall I return there. The Lord gave, and the Lord has taken away; blessed be the name of the Lord." What? After all that had just happened, he praised the Lord? Well, we did read earlier how important it is to praise God in every circumstance, right? Despite all the news Job received, he did not sin or blame God for any of it.

If Job could continue to worship God in spite of all he was going through, how could I possibly get upset about my recent diagnosis? *I should be thankful that I have a dermatologist, that I have health insurance, that I was diagnosed early, that they are keeping me informed and taking care of me—most importantly, that God will take care of me.*

I continued reading. As if losing his family and possessions were not enough, Job's health was attacked next. He was struck with painful boils from head to toe. His skin was shedding. He came down with a fever and chills. He endured itching and swollen limbs, ulcers that were breeding maggots, halitosis, choking, corroding bones, diarrhea, feelings of panic and depression, and terrifying nightmares that led to insomnia. Through all this he still remained faithful to God.

While these hardships brought out the best in Job, they brought out the worst in his wife. She said to her husband, "Do you still hold fast to your integrity? Curse God and die!" (Job 2:9). Unfortunately there are times when those who are closest to us are the ones Satan will use to discourage and divert us from our faith in God.

Job then asked his wife how we can accept good from God and not accept adversity. They go hand in hand like hot and cold, day and night, peanut butter and jelly. Are we to trust God when times are good but not when they're bad? Job's wife failed him when he needed her the most, and he called her a foolish woman for her lack of faith.

The story continues. Although his wife was not able to understand, his three friends came to be with him. They sat with him for an entire week. Grief then overcame Job, and he expressed his feelings to God (remember when I mentioned—that it's okay to yell and complain to get it all out of your system?) He was desperate for rest and healing. God never chastised Job for his expression of grief—but his friends did. They felt Job's outburst was an embarrassment.

The first (and probably Job's oldest) friend, Eliphaz, argued that God punishes the wicked and rewards the righteous, so he assumed sin must be the reason for Job's suffering. Another friend, Bildad, agreed with

Eliphaz and told Job that, if he would just repent for his sins, God would restore him to righteousness. If Job was pure and upright, then God would take care of him. But Job already was pure and upright. Bildad was mistaken regarding the reason for Job's fate. The third friend, Zophar, also urged Job to repent, implying that Job lied about his righteousness. In fact, Zophar felt that God had punished Job more lightly than he deserved.

Can you imagine? Job's friends were not helpful. They had nothing to offer him. His wife had already betrayed him, and now when he needed his friends most, they were abusive and condemning as well.

Job also felt that God was silent and asked why He was hiding His face from Job (13:24). He perceived that God had alienated him, which was more painful than the losses he had already endured. His relationship with God had always meant more to him than anything else. Although God seemed to be silent, Job maintained his innocence and continued to trust God, and he knew he would be vindicated.

In Job 19:14, Job cries out, "My relatives have failed, and my close friends have forgotten me." Wow. I can certainly relate to this one. The pain a person feels when those she loves the most reject her or criticize her can be unbearable. Job had felt the pain of abandonment too, and yet he never gave up on God and a hope for the future. He disputed his friends' claims that the wicked are punished, declaring instead that the wicked prosper even though they mock God and that his friends were naïve to think that only the wicked suffer. The world has proven that this belief is wrong.

Despite all that Job was going through, he always believed God knew his heart, his longings, and his pain and that He cared. Job refused to speak words of wickedness or deceit as long as he lived. Job knew that God had permitted these horrible things to happen to him. He didn't understand why, but he trusted God and knew that his future depended on how he responded to these afflictions.

Sometimes God sends a mediator to help us learn whatever lesson He is teaching us. In Job's case, Elihu presented himself to Job. He proclaimed God's justice, condemned self-righteousness, and proclaimed God's goodness and majesty. God is worthy of our fear and awe because He is God and for no other reason.

Elihu told Job to "stand still and consider the wondrous works of God" (Job 37:14). By doing so, Job prepared himself for God's response. When God revealed Himself to Job, He did not provide him with the reasons for his adversities. He did not give him any answers to his questions. Job was simply reminded of Who was in control.

This encounter with God completely humbled Job, which allowed God to restore him. Job confessed his bitter attitude. God then accused Job's friends of their wrongdoing. He told them that what they had spoken of God was wrong and that Job had spoken rightly. They were ordered to make burnt offerings. When Job prayed for his friends, God restored his losses and even gave him twice as much as he had before. Job's brothers, sisters, and acquaintances returned. They consoled him and comforted him for the adversities he had suffered, and they gave him silver and gold (Job 42:11). As Job grew older, God continued to bless him even more. He again had seven sons and three beautiful daughters. His possessions were multiplied, and he was abundantly blessed beyond what he could have ever imagined.

As I contemplated the story of Job, I knew without a doubt that I would be okay. When we are diagnosed with any kind of illness or disease, especially something terminal, it can be extremely frightening. The skin cancer I had was completely removed, and a few other spots have been removed since. I get regular body scans, and I frequently apply sunblock year-round. There are people far worse off than I am. I'm thankful for having gone through this experience because it's given me a new desire to comfort others and to share my faith with them, even (and especially) when they are facing a more terminal situation. I want them to know they are not alone, and I want them to have the same hope that I gained when I sat still, prayed, and hung on to my faith.

The key to enjoying the blessings you have been given and those that are yet to come is faith—faith that God is always with you, that He loves you, and that He forgives you. Thank Him not for what He does or doesn't give you but for Who He is.

Sorrow and Joy of Ruth

Naomi and her husband lived in the land of Moab with their two sons—Mahlon and Chilion. Naomi's husband died, and her sons were left to care for her. Although both sons had married, they continued to live in the land of Moab and took care of Naomi.

Ten years later both sons died. Naomi's world seemed to be crumbling, but her faith remained intact. Having suffered the loss of her husband and both sons, Naomi decided she would return to her original land of Judah in Israel, where people loved God and God provided for them. She told her two daughters-in-law—Orpah and Ruth—that each should return to her mother's house. Naomi not only grieved for her own losses but for the losses her daughters-in-law suffered as well. She knew, however, that because they were young, they would have a better chance of finding new husbands by returning to their ancestral lands than by staying with Naomi. Orpah, with tears streaming down her face, kissed her mother-in-law and went on her way, but Ruth would not let go of Naomi. Ruth left her own family and the religion of Moab (where idol worship and polygamy were common) and went with Naomi to Bethlehem. Orpah was obedient, but Ruth made a sacrifice.

Understandably, Naomi became bitter, and when they arrived in Bethlehem, she asked the people there not to call her by her name since Naomi meant "pleasant." She asked them to refer to her as Mara, which means "bitter." As Naomi expressed it (Ruth 1:21), "I went out full, and the Lord has brought me home again empty." She may have felt empty physically, but spiritually she was full. Ruth followed Naomi's example as a godly woman. She saw Naomi's perseverance and commitment to keep going, to keep following God, even in the midst of such adversities.

One day it happened that Ruth went out to a field that belonged to a relative of Naomi's late husband. She was gathering grain. This relative, Boaz, was both godly and wealthy. He also went out to the field. When he saw Ruth, he asked whom she belonged to. In other words, he wanted to know if she was married or single.

The servant in charge explained to Boaz that she had returned with Naomi and had been gathering grain all day.

I can imagine how Ruth must have looked—tired, dirty, hair all a mess—but Boaz was drawn to her. He respected her. He warned the other men not to touch her, and he offered her water, which the young men had drawn. Boaz knew all that Ruth had done for her mother-in-law after the loss of their loved ones. He knew that she left her own father and mother and her birthplace and came to a land and people she didn't know. Boaz saw her honesty, integrity, and commitment.

Boaz invited Ruth to dinner and served the best meal he could offer. She ate plenty and even had enough left over to take with her (God not only provides our needs, He gives abundantly). Boaz later told the servants in the fields to purposely let bundles of barley and wheat fall so that Ruth might gather it up. She gathered enough to feed two people for an entire week.

Naomi asked Ruth where she had been gathering the grain and with whom she had worked. When Ruth told her it was Boaz, Naomi was pleased to inform her that he was a close relative and asked the Lord to bless him for his kindness. She also told Ruth to stay close by the young women of Boaz. Ruth honored her vow to Naomi and did as she was told until the end of the harvest season.

Knowing that Boaz and Ruth were attracted to one another, Naomi arranged for Ruth to go to Boaz and gain his attention. She asked for his protection. He was pleased with her kindness and agreed to take care of her. He even let her know that all the townspeople knew her as a virtuous woman. She lay at his feet all night just as he asked.

Just before the sun rose, he sent her home with more barley, not wanting her to return to her mother-in-law empty-handed. Naomi predicted that Boaz would make a decision regarding Ruth before the end of the day. Sure enough, Boaz went to the place where legal matters were settled and bought the land that belonged to Naomi and her sons. By doing so, he also acquired Ruth as his wife.

Ruth (Gentile) and Boaz (Hebrew) had a son, and they named him Obed. Obed became the father of Jesse. Jesse was the father of David, the future king. Ruth was the great-grandmother of King David, and King David was prominent in the lineage of the Messiah.

Naomi and Ruth grieved, and God brought them comfort. This comfort helped them to stay committed to one another and to God. Because of their commitment and steady faith, God blessed them. Ruth was an ordinary young lady, and God used her for a great purpose. Because of the faithfulness of these two women, God provided food, security, posterity, and eventually the Messiah through the lineage of Ruth and Boaz.

We all experience loss and grieving from time to time. Don't let this lead you to turn your back on God. Stay committed. Follow His lead, and do what you know in your heart is right regardless of how difficult it may be. You might be the next ordinary person God uses for a great purpose.

Imprisonment and
Power of Joseph

People in biblical times were imprisoned just like people today, sometimes rightly and sometimes even when innocent because of flaws in our judicial system. Actually, it was probably worse in biblical times. They didn't have televisions, social time, gym equipment, or hot meals as most prisons have today.

Jeremiah, a prophet, was attacked by his brothers, beaten by a priest and false prophet, and confined to a muddy dungeon by the king—all because they didn't like that he was preaching and pointing out their sins and telling them these sins were the reasons for impending disaster. The dungeon was so deep that he had to be lowered into it by rope. The mud was so thick, his feet sank. He remained there with no water and only one piece of bread a day. He was sure to die until Nebuchadnezzar seized Jerusalem and demanded that Jeremiah be lifted out of the dungeon. (See Jeremiah 37 & 38)

Two other preachers, Paul and Silas, commanded an evil spirit to depart from a young girl. When her owners found out, they were angry because they could no longer make a profit off her. So Paul and Silas were beaten and thrown in jail. While in jail, they continued to preach to other prisoners. Even the family who owned the jail became saved and baptized because of their preaching. They didn't belong in jail, but because they found themselves in that situation, they used it for good by telling others there about God. (See Acts 16:16—34)

John the Baptist was also imprisoned. He had said to Herod (see Mark 6:18), "It is not lawful for you to have your brother's wife." This wife was Herodias. So Herod became angry, seized John the Baptist, and threw him in jail.

During Herod's birthday celebration, Herodias's daughter danced for him. He was so pleased that he offered to give her anything she desired. She asked her mother what to request, and her mother said, "The head of John the Baptist!" So the daughter asked for his head on a platter (you can't make this stuff up; see Mark 6:22–29). Although Herod had John the Baptist imprisoned, he knew he was a holy man. Still, he ordered his beheading so as not to break his promise to the daughter of Herodias.

Although John the Baptist was never released from prison and instead was murdered, he was a godly man when his life ended. He had lived a blessed life. He baptized Jesus. He introduced Jesus to the disciples as the "Lamb of God." Jesus even regarded John as "a burning and shining lamp" (John 5:35). He had served his purpose as a man who loved the Lord, and this pleased God.

Joseph was the youngest of Jacob's sons but one, the older son of Jacob's beloved Rachel, and because of this he was also the most loved by his father. This caused his brothers to hate him. They would not even speak nicely to him. One night Joseph dreamed that he would be greatly blessed. He would rule over a land and its people and they would bow down to him. Even his brothers would bow down to him. He shared this dream with his brothers, and this made them hate him even more (Genesis 37:5).

One day his father sent Joseph to check on his brothers who were feeding the flock. Joseph had no idea that they were conspiring to kill him. They planned to tell their father he was devoured by a wild beast. When one of the brothers, Reuben, heard their plan, he convinced them not to kill him but to throw him into a pit (this way Reuben could later rescue him). So Joseph's brothers stripped him and tossed him into a pit.

While they were taking a break and eating, they saw the Ishmaelites coming and decided to sell Joseph to them to become their slave. Reuben then gathered up Joseph's clothes from the pit and tore them. The brothers killed a goat and dipped Joseph's torn clothes into the goat's blood. They took the bloody torn shreds of clothing to their father, saying they found them. Jacob recognized these strips of material as Joseph's, and he mourned the loss of his son. He was so distraught that he would not allow his own family to comfort him. He went down to the grave of his son (probably the pit where he was supposedly devoured) and cried.

Meanwhile, the Ishmaelites who had bought Joseph from his brothers took him to Egypt. Potiphar, an officer of Pharaoh, bought Joseph from the Ishmaelites. Because Joseph served his master well, he was made the overseer of the Egyptian's house. God took care of Joseph, and Joseph respected his master.

One day while no one was around, his master's wife tried to seduce him, but Joseph refused because she was his master's wife. She continued these antics until one day she grabbed hold of his garment and tried once again to seduce him. With his garment still in her hand, he ran from her. She lied and told the men of her house that Joseph came to mock her, and when she yelled for help, he fled. Joseph's master believed her and became angry with Joseph. He took Joseph and confined him to prison.

While he was in prison, he interpreted the dreams of two inmates, a butler and a baker. Joseph explained to the butler that according to his dream, in three days Pharaoh would again make him his butler. Joseph asked that he remember him and mention him to Pharaoh so that he might be freed from prison, since he was innocent. Joseph then explained to the baker that according to his dream, in three days he would be hanged from a tree, and the birds would eat his flesh. Three days later, the baker was hanged, and the butler was restored to his post, but he did not remember Joseph.

Two years later, Joseph still remained an innocent man in prison. Pharaoh had a dream. He shared his dream with the butler and said he didn't understand what it meant. The butler now remembered Joseph and told Pharaoh about him. So Pharaoh sent for Joseph and asked him to interpret his dream. Joseph explained that according to his dream, there would be seven years of plenty throughout the land of Egypt followed by seven years of severe famine. Of course, Pharaoh's dream would also come to be true. Pharaoh made Joseph governor of the land and ruler over all his people. During the years of plenty, Joseph gathered up immeasurable amounts of grain so that he could feed the people in the land of Egypt. (During this time he married and had two sons.) When the years of famine began, Egypt was the only land with bread, and Joseph was in charge of selling it to those who offered to buy it.

Jacob, Joseph's father, heard that Egypt had grain available and sent his sons to buy some. When they arrived, Joseph recognized them as his brothers, but they did not recognize him. They bowed before him—just as Joseph had dreamed many years earlier. He pretended not to know them and asked where they were from. They answered. Then Joseph cited a dream he had about them and accused them of being spies who had come to see the nakedness of the land. They denied this accusation, saying that they had come to buy food and were all one man's sons and honest men, not spies.

They told Joseph that their youngest brother, Benjamin, had stayed behind with their father, and another brother was dead. Joseph told them they needed to be tested to prove they weren't spies, so he sent his brothers to prison for three days and said that Benjamin must come for them, or they would not be freed. On the third day he let all but one brother go and take grain back to their land, and they were told to bring Benjamin to him to verify the truth of their claim. They now confessed to one another their guilt in what they had done to Joseph (they still did not realize he was the Egyptian official) and knew they were in this predicament because of what they had done, for this was their punishment. They left their brother Simeon behind in prison and returned to their land of Canaan.

When they returned home and opened their sacks, not only did they have grain but they also had money in their sacks, and they didn't understand it. They explained to their father, Jacob, what had happened, and he was grieved. He said to them in Genesis 42:36, "Joseph is no more, Simeon is no more, and you want to take Benjamin? All these things are against me." Reuben told his father to kill his own two sons if he did not bring Benjamin back as promised, but Jacob refused. They remained in the land of Canaan, and after the grain was gone that Joseph had given them, their father asked them to go buy more.

They returned to Egypt with Benjamin, money to buy the grain (the money they had found in their sacks after the first trip), and a gift for Joseph. The men of

Joseph's house gave them water to wash their feet and feed for their donkeys. Joseph prepared a meal for them in his house, asked about the well-being of their father, and met Benjamin, his younger brother. His heart yearned for his younger brother, Benjamin, and he left the room to cry.

Later, when they were ready to leave, Joseph again had their sacks filled with money as well as grain. He also had his own silver cup placed in Benjamin's sack. The silver cup was a divine object, and it was common practice in Egypt to disturb the water in the silver cup with a drop of oil or a coin and interpret the resulting patterns in the water. The penalty for theft of such a divine object was typically death. By placing the cup in Benjamin's sack, Joseph was testing his brothers' attitude toward Benjamin.

When Benjamin was caught with the silver cup, Joseph said he would take Benjamin to be his slave and the rest of them should return to their father. They explained to Joseph that if they returned without Benjamin, their father would surely die. They explained to Joseph everything that had happened. When Joseph could no longer withhold his true identity as their brother, he finally confessed to them who he was. They were speechless, but Joseph told them not to be grieved or angry because their selling him into slavery had worked out for good. God had protected him in the pit and in prison. God allowed him to be sold into slavery and later made him a ruler so that he could provide for them now.

If God can take Joseph's situation—hated by his brothers, object of a murder plot, thrown into a pit, sold into slavery, wrongly accused and imprisoned—and turn it around for something so powerful and good in the future, don't you think He can do the same for you in whatever situation you're facing?

Survival and Deliverance of Daniel

Daniel was an older man—perhaps in his eighties—and a governor in his time. He was also honorable and faithful to God. The other governors didn't like that they could not find fault with him, no matter how hard they tried. So they devised a plan and tricked Darius, who was in charge of the governors, into decreeing that no one could petition any god or man for thirty days or he would be cast into the den of lions. Daniel heard of this decree but remained committed to God, even though he knew it would mean punishment for disobeying the decree.

It was his custom to kneel and pray three times a day giving thanks to God. When the governors caught him praying, they went before the king and informed them of what Daniel had done. They exclaimed that Daniel did not show due regard for the king or the decree and must be punished. The king was saddened by this, but no decree or statute of the Medes and Persians could be changed.

Daniel was thrown into the lion's den at sundown. In Daniel 6:16, the king said to Daniel, "Your God, whom you serve continually, He will deliver you." The king was so concerned about Daniel that he did not sleep that night. He got up very early in the morning and rushed to the den to check on him. When he arrived, he cried tears of joy to see that Daniel was still very much alive. Daniel said to him in verse 22, "My God sent His angel and shut the lions' mouths, so that they have not hurt me, because I was found innocent before Him; and also, O king, I have done no wrong before you." The king had him removed from the lion's den. He had no injury whatsoever because he believed in God and God protected him.

The king ordered Daniel's accusers to be brought to him. He then cast them and their families into the lions' den. Before they even reached the back of the den, they were devoured by the lions. Because of these things,

King Darius wrote a new decree that in every dominion of his kingdom men must tremble in fear before the God of Daniel. Part of this decree stated, "He delivers and rescues, and He works signs and wonders in heaven and on earth, Who has delivered Daniel from the power of the lions" (verses 26–27).

Maybe someone has tricked you. Or perhaps someone just doesn't like you for whatever reason. They try to make you look bad because they can't find any obvious fault with you. Maybe you have found yourself suddenly surrounded by a pack of ferocious lions. Are you afraid and waiting for them to devour you? Or are you faithful and confident that God will deliver you from your lions' den?

Confidence and
Victory of David

The Philistines massed their armies on a mountain for war against Israel. Saul and the men of Israel gathered on the opposite mountain, and between them was a valley. Goliath, the champion of the Philistines, was a giant who stood some nine feet tall. His armor consisted of a bronze helmet, a two-hundred-pound coat, bronze armor on his legs, and a bronze javelin between his shoulders. His iron spearhead alone weighed twenty pounds, and before him he held a shield.

He mocked Saul and his men and said if they would send someone to kill him, then his army would become their servants. Saul and his men became afraid when they heard this. Saul forfeited the opportunity to fight Goliath because he was only relying on himself instead of having faith that God would give him victory. He went cowering into the tent, which was not God's will.

Meanwhile, David was working in the field (doing God's will). His father, Jesse, told him to take grain and cheese to his brothers fighting in the battle, see how they were doing, and report back. So David, the youngest brother and still just a boy, left the sheep and supplies with a keeper and ran to the army camp. He greeted his brothers and asked how they were doing. They told him about the giant Goliath and how afraid they were. David interrupted them and asked what would be done for the man who killed the giant who defied the armies of the living God. (This was something Saul, as head of the army, should have asked.) They answered and told David that whoever killed the giant would gain the giant's army as their servants.

David's brother Eliab became angry with him and asked him what he had done with the sheep he was caring for. He accused David of leaving the sheep behind and coming to the mountain just to see the battle. David defended himself and asked (1 Samuel 17:29), "What have I done now? Is there not a cause?" (Many translations render the second part as, "It was only a question!") When others heard David's conversation with his brothers, they reported this to Saul, and Saul sent for him.

David then said to Saul (verse 32), "Let no man's heart fail because of him; your servant will go and fight with this Philistine." But Saul told David he could not fight the giant because he was just a kid. David explained how he had been protecting the sheep, and whenever a lion or bear came and took a lamb from the flock, he went out after it and struck it and delivered the lamb from its mouth, and when the lion or bear arose against him, he caught it by its beard and struck and killed it (verse 35). He saw the giant as a lion or bear, but above all, he said, "The Lord, who delivered me from the paw of the lion and from the paw of the bear, He will deliver me from the hand of this Philistine" (verse 37). So Saul allowed him to go to battle with the giant and prayed that the Lord would be with him.

Saul clothed David in his armor and put a bronze helmet on his head. David fastened his sword to his armor and tried to walk, since he had never tested this armor before. He told Saul, "I cannot walk with these," (verse 39) and took them off. Instead of the sword, David took his sling and five smooth stones from the brook. He put them in a shepherd's bag, a small pouch, and advanced toward the giant, who advanced on his part.

The giant then said to David (verse 43), "Am I a dog that you come to me with sticks?" He cursed David and told him he would give his flesh to the birds and beasts.

But David was not afraid. He spoke to the giant, saying,

> You come to me with a sword, a spear, and a javelin. But I come to you in the name of the Lord of hosts, the God of the armies of Israel, whom you have defied. This day the Lord will deliver you into my hand and I will strike you and take your head from you. And this day I will give the carcasses of the camp of the Philistines to the birds and the beasts that all the earth may know that there is a God in Israel. Then all this assembly shall know that the Lord does not save with sword and spear, for the battle is the Lord's, and He will give you into our hands. (verses 45–47)

When the giant approached him, David reached into his bag, pulled out a smooth stone, and slung it at the giant. It struck the giant's forehead and sank into his flesh. The giant fell to the ground on his face. The giant had been killed with a sling and stone, but there was no sword in David's hand. So "David ran and stood over the Philistine, took his sword and drew it out of its sheath and killed him, and cut off his head" (verse 51). When the Philistines saw that their champion was dead, they fled. The men of Israel and Judah went after them, killing and wounding many before returning to their camp.

David, young and small, went up against the giant Goliath. But David knew his God was far bigger than this giant. He did not focus on the giant in front of him but on the fact that Goliath was confronting God rather than David. He knew God would protect him and give him victory.

Will you allow your situation to define you, or will you define your situation? Confidence is the key ingredient for creating victory. One of my favorite Bible verses is 1 John 5:4: "Whatever is born of God overcomes the world. And this is the victory that has overcome the world—our faith." Faith brings confidence, which creates victory.

Patience and Peacemaking
of Abigail

There was a man named Nabal. He was very rich and owned thousands of sheep and goats. Unfortunately he was harsh, evil, and overbearing. Nabal's shepherds had been with David and his people in Carmel. The shepherds were taken care of by David and his people. So at a later time when David heard that Nabal was in the wilderness shearing his sheep, he asked his men to go to Nabal in peace and request a favor in return on this feast day. Nabal answered David's servants (1 Samuel 25:10–11) by saying, "Who is David, and who is the son of Jesse? There are many servants nowadays who break away each one from his master." Now notice how self-centered Nabal is when he continues his response: "Shall *I* then take *my* bread and *my* water and *my* meat that *I* have killed for *my* shearers, and give it to men when *I* do not know where they are from?"

When David's men returned this message to him, David told them to get their swords. How could this evil person whose shepherds were cared for by David and his people now be so cruel? David planned to kill him for his harsh attitude. About four hundred men went with David after Nabal. One of the shepherds went to Abigail, Nabal's wife, and told her what had happened. He explained that David and his men had been good to the shepherds, but Nabal was rude and would not return the favor. He warned Abigail that David and his men were returning to harm Nabal and his household. Referring to Nabal (verse 17), he said, "For he is such a scoundrel that one cannot speak to him."

Abigail was understanding, intelligent, patient, and beautiful. Most likely she did not choose Nabal as her husband. Her marriage to this difficult man was probably arranged by her parents, which was common in those days. Knowing that her husband would not listen to her and that she had to do something to protect her household, she alone gathered up bread, wine, sheep, grain, raisins, and fig cakes and loaded them onto donkeys. She had her servants go ahead of her, and she did not tell Nabal what she was doing. She rode on the donkey and eventually met up with David and all his men who were heading toward her. She dismounted the donkey and fell to her face at his feet. She took the blame for her husband's horrible behavior and begged David's forgiveness, offering him all that she had gathered and brought with her. She displayed confidence when she explained to him that the Lord was holding him back from coming to bloodshed by sending her to him. By stopping him from committing murder, she was ensuring that God would be pleased with him, and she asked that he remember her for doing so.

David replied (verses 32–33), "Blessed is the Lord God of Israel, who sent you this day to meet me! And blessed is your advice and blessed are you, because you have kept me this day from coming to bloodshed and from avenging myself with my own hand." He took her advice because he respected her for what she had done; then he sent her home in peace.

When she arrived home, she found Nabal having a party. He was very drunk so she did not tell him anything about what had happened. The following morning when he was finally sober, Abigail, willing to accept any consequence, told him what had happened, and his heart was hardened. He was a cold, harsh man. Ten days later, the Lord struck Nabal, and he died.

David heard of Nabal's death and realized that the Lord had returned the wickedness of Nabal on his own head. Vengeance belongs to God. He will take care of things in His own way and in His own time. Now that Nabal was no more, David proposed to Abigail, and she gladly accepted. The Lord blessed them both—David for not taking matters into his own hands, and Abigail for showing courage, wisdom, and respect.

If you are stuck in a difficult situation, position, or relationship, as Abigail was, I encourage you to ask God to take care of it. Ask Him how you should handle it, and do as he instructs, always being kind and understanding along the way. Let God handle the consequences of any person who has wronged either you or someone else. That's His job, not yours.

Conclusion

The Bible is filled with stories of people overcoming adversities. God tells us we will face trials and tribulations. But He also promises to be with us during these times. He gives us the resources we need to find joy in the midst of sorrow and suffering, to gain power when we feel trapped, to deliver us in frightening times, and to enjoy victory.

We are told in Psalm 37:3–4, "Trust in the Lord, and do good; dwell in the land, and feed on His faithfulness. Delight yourself also in the Lord, and He shall give you the desires of your heart." God loves us and cares for us. He provides all our needs. He knows what's best for us and when it's best for us.

God gives us hope, strength, and comfort as tools to carry us through the adversities of life. His Word is full of instruction. He has given us the information we need in order to handle every situation we might face. He also listens when we call out to Him for answers and guidance. He loves us more than we can fathom.

He also blesses us in countless ways, big and small. It's easy to begin taking these blessings for granted. We get comfortable, even complacent. It's important to stop once in a while and think about all we have to be thankful for—from the first flower that peeks out of the spring soil to the warm mittens on our hands under the falling snow, from the giggle of an innocent child to the sincere smile of a thankful neighbor. When the trials of today begin to discourage us, we must remember all that we've been blessed with and embrace the future that God so intensely wants to give us.

Appendix

Each time you think of something (big or small) that you are thankful for, some way that you have been blessed, write it down. Look at it often, especially when you start to feel discouraged.

1. _____
2. _____
3. _____
4. _____
5. _____
6. _____
7. _____
8. _____
9. _____

10. _____
11. _____
12. _____
13. _____
14. _____
15. _____
16. _____
17. _____
18. _____
19. _____
20. _____
21. _____
22. _____
23. _____
24. _____
25. _____
26. _____
27. _____
28. _____
29. _____
30. _____
31. _____
32. _____
33. _____
34. _____
35. _____

36. _____

37. _____

38. _____

39. _____

40. _____

41. _____

42. _____

43. _____

44. _____

45. _____

46. _____

47. _____

48. _____

49. _____

50. _____

51. _____

52. _____

53. _____

54. _____

55. _____

56. _____

57. _____

58. _____

59. _____

60. _____

61. _____

62. _____
63. _____
64. _____
65. _____
66. _____
67. _____
68. _____
69. _____
70. _____
71. _____
72. _____
73. _____
74. _____
75. _____
76. _____
77. _____
78. _____
79. _____
80. _____
81. _____
82. _____
83. _____
84. _____
85. _____
86. _____
87. _____

88. _____

89. _____

90. _____

91. _____

92. _____

93. _____

94. _____

95. _____

96. _____

97. _____

98. _____

99. _____

100. _____